A Note to Parents and Teachers

Discovery Readers are nonfiction books designed for the beginning reader. Each Discovery Reader is filled with informative text, short sentences, and colorful and whimsical illustrations.

Discovery Readers make nonfiction subjects fun and historical subjects come alive. But nonfiction stories must use some words that cannot be changed for easier ones. For this reason, we encourage you to help the child with the short vocabulary list below before he or she begins the book. Learning these words will make reading the story easier.

Vocabulary List

Benjamin	New York
Franklin	Philadelphia
Boston	America
Massachusetts	Declaration
England	Independence
Josiah	France
James	French
Silence	Constitution
Dogood	

ISBN 0-8249-5509-9

Published by Ideals Children's Books
An imprint of Ideals Publications
A division of Guideposts
535 Metroplex Drive, Suite 250
Nashville, Tennessee 37211
www.idealsbooks.com

R.L. 2.5 Spache

Library of Congress Cataloging-in-Publication Data

Pingry, Patricia A., date.
  Discover Benjamin Franklin / written by Patricia A. Pingry ;
illustrated by Stephanie McFetridge Britt.
    p. cm. — (Discovery readers)
  ISBN 0-8249-5509-9 (alk. paper)
1. Franklin, Benjamin, 1706-1790—Juvenile literature.
2. Statesmen—United States—Biography Juvenile literature.
3. Inventors—United States—Biography—Juvenile literature.
4. Scientists—United States—Biography—Juvenile literature.
5. Printers—United States—Biography—Juvenile literature. I.
Britt, Stephanie, ill. II. Title. III. Series.
  E302.6.F8P6155 2005
  973.3'092—dc22

                              2005010910

Printed in Italy by LEGO

10 9 8 7 6 5 4 3 2 1

Designed by Jenny Eber Hancock

For Ben Pingry

Discover
BENJAMIN FRANKLIN

PRINTER • SCIENTIST • STATESMAN

WRITTEN BY PATRICIA A. PINGRY

ILLUSTRATED BY STEPHANIE MCFETRIDGE BRITT

ideals children's books

Nashville, Tennessee

Benjamin Franklin was
born on January 17, 1706
in Boston, Massachusetts.
He had nine brothers and
thirteen sisters!

Ben learned to read
when he was only
three years old.

There was only one
book in Ben's house.

So Ben read the Bible
from beginning to end.
Then he read it again.

Ben went to school
for two years.

Then he had to quit
and help his father, Josiah,
in his candle shop.

Ben and his family lived
over the candle shop.
Candlelight was the only
light people had.

Ben cut wicks for the
candles. He filled the
molds with melted wax.

He ran errands
for his dad.

He sold candles.
But Ben did not like
the candle shop.
Ben loved the sea.

Josiah was afraid that
Ben might run away
and become a sailor.

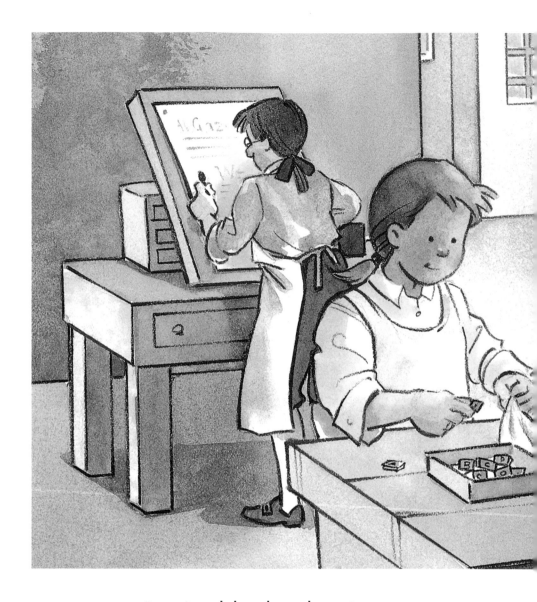

Ben's older brother James
had a print shop. Josiah
asked James if Ben could
work for him.

Ben set the type for the
newspaper. He read the
stories. He checked the
spelling. Ben did a good job.

Ben began to write
articles. He signed them
"Silence Dogood." He
slid them under the door
of the print shop.

James thought the articles
were good. He printed
them in the newspaper.
He did not know that
Ben wrote them.

Ben lived with James. One
day, Ben asked James to
give him half the money
spent on him. This would
save his brother some money.

Now Ben slept in the print
shop. He spent half of his
money on food. He bought
books with the rest. Ben often
stayed up all night reading.

Ben still loved the water.
Ben taught himself to swim.
Most people in Boston
did not know how to swim.

So Ben taught his friends
how to swim.

Ben also loved science. One day, Ben went for a swim in the pond. He lay on his back in the water.

He held the string of a kite. The kite pulled him all across the pond!

When Ben was seventeen,
he wanted to leave the
print shop. But his father
had promised that Ben
would stay for nine years.
Ben ran away.

Ben sold some of his
books. He bought a ticket
to New York. But in New
York, there were no jobs
for printers. So Ben went
to Philadelphia.

When Ben got off the
boat, he had one dollar
and a few cents. He
was tired and dirty. He
was also very hungry.

Ben bought three
loaves of bread
for three pennies.

He gave some to a
hungry woman and
her child.

Ben found work as a printer. Then he bought his own print shop and started a newspaper.

Ben wanted all people to have books. So Ben began the first library in America.

He developed a stove
that gave more heat
than a fireplace.

He invented lightning
rods so lightning would
not burn down buildings.

One night, Ben flew a
kite in the rain. Ben
tied a key to the kite.

24

When lightning struck
the key, Ben proved that
lightning was electricity.

In 1775, Ben helped
draw up the Declaration of
Independence. This would
mean war with England.

Ben signed the Declaration
of Independence anyway.
It was the right thing to do.

Ben went to France to
ask for help in the war.
The French loved Ben.
They sent their navy to help.

Ben kept inventing things. He
needed eyeglasses. He used
one pair to read. Another
pair helped him see far away.

28

So Ben invented bifocals.
Now he only needed one
pair of glasses to help him
read and see far away.

In 1785, Ben came home
from France. A band
played. Crowds cheered.

Ben was seventy-nine years old. Now he helped write the U.S. Constitution.

To honor Ben, we put his picture on the one-hundred-dollar bill.

Ben was a printer and scientist. He helped America gain her independence.

But most of all, Ben loved helping people.